THIS YEARBOOK BELONGS TO...

CHARLOTTE Dujardin YEARBOOK

P26

P30

Published by DJ Murphy (Publishers) Ltd, Marlborough House, Headley Road, Grayshott, Surrey GU26 6LG

Who did what in this Yearbook

With thanks to Charlotte Dujardin, Abby Newell at Piaffe, Rose Lewis at Daydream Photography, Alan Davies, Equisafety, Charles Owen, Kingsland, LeMieux, Dressage Anywhere, Horsepower/Olympia/Windsor Horse Show
Contributors Jo Browne, Kiera Boyle, Megan Hurley, Bethany Searby, Janet Dashley-Payne, Jessica Matthews
Art Editor Sarah Garland
Designers Jake Booth, Lizzi Porter, Adam Witt
Cover and feature photography Daydream Photography
Additional photography Jon Stroud, Jess Photography, Scott Matthews, Shutterstock/ Neale Cousland/Gracethang2
Managing Director Zoe Cannon
Commercial Director Abi Cannon

The Charlotte Dujardin Yearbook is produced under license by DJ Murphy (Publishers) Ltd. © Copyright DJ Murphy (Publishers) Ltd.

Printed by TJ Books, Padstow, Cornwall

ISBN 978-1-913787-02-8

P10

P40

TIME OF *my life*

Follow my journey to Olympic success

13 July 1985
Charlotte Susan Jane Dujardin is born in Enfield, Middlesex!

1987
Aged two I have my first ride on a pony, a mare called Sovereign.

1988
My first Pony Club showjumping competition's a successful one, and I'm placed second.

1996
Winning a championship at the Royal International Horse Show with Ardenhall Royal Secret is one of my most memorable moments.

2001
After several amazing years in showing, I switch disciplines and decide to specialise in dressage.

> In a dream come true, I'm chosen to ride for Great Britain

2007
Such an important year for me! I arrive at Carl Hester's yard, sit on Valegro for the first time and start competing him.

2011
In a dream come true, I'm chosen to ride for Great Britain at the 2011 European Dressage Champs in Rotterdam. Thanks to performances by Valegro and my team-mates Carl Hester, Emile Faurie and Laura Tomlinson we're team gold medallists.

2008
Valegro and I are National Champions at Elementary and Medium levels.

2012
Can life get any better? Valegro and I win individual and team gold at London 2012, then top off an incredible year winning the World Cup Freestyle at Olympia.

> **There are more medal celebrations at Rio 2016**

2013
I'm honoured to receive an OBE at Buckingham Palace for my services to equestrianism.

2015
We win the FEI World Cup final in Las Vegas, USA, and are European Champions for the second time.

2014
Valegro impresses the judges at the World Equestrian Games in Normandy, France, and we're crowned World Champions. We also set a new record in the Grand Prix Freestyle at Olympia, scoring a massive 94.3%

2016
There are more medal celebrations at Rio 2016. This time I take home an individual gold and team silver.

2016
After Rio, we make the difficult decision to retire Valegro from competition. We perform our last dance together in an emotional retirement ceremony at Olympia Horse Show.

2018
I cement my new partnership with Mount St John Freestyle by winning a team bronze medal at the World Equestrian Games, held in Tryon, USA.

2019
I get the perfect Christmas present at Olympia when Freestyle and I triumph in the dressage to music.

2017
I'm invited to Buckingham Palace again, this time to receive a CBE. Mum and Dad come to the ceremony with me.

2020
Competition plans may have been interrupted this year, but Freestyle and I show we're still on top form by winning the Hickstead Rotterdam Grand Prix Challenge.

9

Brilliant
BLUEBERRY

Celebrating the most famous horse in the world – Valegro

FACT FILE
Name: Valegro
Stable name: Blueberry
Foaled: 2002
Colour: Dark bay
Breed: Dutch Warmblood, by Negro
Height: 16.2hh
Owned by: Carl Hester, Rowena Luard and Anne Barrott
Fast fact: He's my best friend, as well as my horse of a lifetime. I love him more than words can say.

Valegro – aka Blueberry – is my horse of a lifetime. He's helped me achieve more than I ever could have imagined, and even now it's quite hard to believe that we danced our way to three Olympic gold medals, and broke several world records along the way. Wow – what an incredible horse! You're sure to know loads about him already, but let me talk you through his story, from how it all started to what he's been getting up to in his retirement.

Talent spotting
Carl first spotted a two-year-old Valegro in 2004 at a stallion event in The Netherlands, and he bought him for just £4,000. He could tell this was a special horse, but for a while Valegro's future was uncertain because Carl didn't think he was big enough to make a dressage star.

I first got to ride Blueberry when I went to work for Carl in 2007. He's a powerful, buzzy horse – exactly the type I love – and we clicked straight away. From then on, I just wanted to prove to the dressage world what Blueberry could really do.

History in the making
It wasn't long before Blueberry and I became a winning partnership. Both his attitude and his ability were second to none, and he wowed the judges at every competition we went to. We sailed through all the dressage levels, and began competing abroad, too, which was an incredible experience.

Carl and I never really discussed Blueberry's future, and everyone – including me – thought that he would take over the ride and compete him at Grand Prix. So, I was surprised and delighted when Carl gave me the opportunity of a lifetime – the chance to aim for the London 2012 Olympics with Blueberry!

Everyone wants to meet Blueberry!

 We clicked straight away and I wanted to prove to the dressage world what Blueberry could really do

DID YOU KNOW?
Blueberry's fave dressage move was one-time changes. He was really good at them and judges often gave him a 10!

11

ROLL OF HONOUR

- Individual gold and team silver, 2016 Rio Olympics

- Individual gold, Grand Prix Special and Freestyle, 2015 European Championships, Aachen, Germany

- 1st, FEI World Cup Dressage Finals 2015, Las Vegas, USA

- Individual gold, Grand Prix Special and Freestyle, 2014 World Equestrian Games, Normandy, France

- Individual gold, Grand Prix Special and Freestyle, and Bronze team medal, 2013 European Championships, Herning, Denmark

- Team and individual gold, 2012 London Olympics

Going for gold

In one of the most memorable moments of my career, Blueberry and I were selected to ride for Team GB at the London 2012 Olympics, where we clinched team and individual gold. Four years later, we were crowned Olympic champions again at Rio, and took home a team silver medal, too. Blueberry is amazing, and always made me feel I could do anything!

DID YOU KNOW?
I've never ever fallen off Blueberry!

Best of friends

Blueberry and I have a super-strong bond. We know each other inside out and I absolutely adore all his cheeky little ways. Here are a few fun facts about him that you might not have heard before...

- his fave thing's eating! From grabbing a cheeky snack out on a hack to asking everyone for treats, Blueberry loves nothing more than food, and sugar cubes are his absolute fave
- another of Blueberry's best pals is our groom Alan Davies. They have an amazing bond
- Blueberry's as laidback as they come, and is really chilled out hacking, but he was quite hot to ride when we were competing and always had lots of energy
- he's a born performer and was never spooky at a competition. He was never phased by flower pots, banners or huge crowds
- Blueberry has such a nice temperament and adores cuddles. It's why everyone on the yard loves him

DID YOU KNOW?

Valegro has his own series of novels! The Blueberry stories tell the tale of his rise to fame in his own words!

Time to say goodbye at Olympia 2016

Well-earned retirement

By the time he was 14, Blueberry had won everything there was to win, so Carl, his other owners and I made the decision to retire him from competition. He bowed out in a special ceremony at Olympia in 2016, just a few months after the Rio Olympics. It was incredibly emotional and there wasn't a dry eye in the house!

Since then, Blueberry's been enjoying a quieter life at Carl's yard, although he still has a pretty busy schedule. He's ridden several times a week, enjoying regular hacks, and he helps teach trainee riders all the moves he was famous for. He makes a few public appearances every year, too. As you can imagine, the fans absolutely adore him and the meet-and-greet queue is always super-long!

DRESSAGE *A-Z*

All you need to know about riding between the boards

A
is for Aids

Your aids are your voice, legs, reins and seat when you use them to communicate with your pony. They help him understand what you want him to do, whether that's change pace, turn to the left or right or move sideways in lateral work. In dressage it's super-important that he responds to your aids as soon as you ask him to do something. It'll impress the judge and help you score higher marks.

B
is for Bell

This lets you know it's time to begin your test. When it's your turn and the steward sends you over to the dressage arena, you'll need to ride around the white boards until the judge is ready. When they are, they'll ring the bell. You'll then have 45 seconds to turn down the centre line, so don't hang about!

C
is for Collectives

At the bottom of your dressage score sheet you'll see four or five extra boxes which are called the collective marks. This is where the judge scores your overall performance in the test, including your pony's paces, impulsion and responsiveness, and your position and effectiveness as a rider. The collectives can be super-important to your final score because these marks are often doubled. If there's a tie, the rider with the higher collective marks wins!

D
is for Double bridle

Double bridles are used in the higher levels of dressage to enhance the communication a rider has with their horse. A double bridle has two bits and two pairs of reins. You hold the snaffle rein as normal with your thumbs on top, and the curb rein goes between your second and third fingers.

E
is for European Champs

This championship is where the best dressage riders in Europe compete for medals! It's held every other year and competitors are chosen to ride for their country as an individual or on a team. They're amazing events to be involved in, and Valegro and I have won seven medals at three European Champs!

F
is for Flying change

This is a super-cool way to change direction! It's when you change canter lead in mid-air, and there'll be a moment of suspension when all four of your pony's legs are off the ground! It looks very impressive, but you won't be asked to perform one in a test until you reach the more advanced levels.

G
is for Grand Prix

Welcome to the very pinnacle of dressage competition! There are three different types of test you can ride at this level – Grand Prix, Grand Prix Special and Grand Prix Freestyle, and Valegro and I have set the world record for all of them! The tests include really awesome moves that take lots of practice to perfect. They're quite long, too, as so many movements are included!

H
is for Halt

The halt is a really important thing to ace! Even though your pony will be standing still, you'll need to show the judge that he's obedient enough to halt square. In higher-level dressage tests you halt and salute twice – at the beginning, then again at the end. When you practise your halts at home, ask someone to watch you to check that your pony's standing square on all four legs!

I
is for Inside bend

When you ride a circle, a corner or any other move that follows a curve, your pony should have a soft bend through his body. To ask him to bend, open your inside rein a little and press your inside leg on the girth. You'll know it's right when you can just see the corner of his inside eye.

is for Judge

This is the person you'll need to impress with your awesome dressage moves! One judge always sits at C, but when I'm competing in a major championship there could be up to seven judges positioned all around the arena. This is so they can rate the horse's paces and your riding from every possible angle!

K
is for Keep smiling

If you get a little nervous before a test, a great way to stay calm is to smile! Smiling can naturally trick your brain into thinking there's nothing to worry about. Plus, it's a fab way to show the judge you're enjoying yourself and feeling confident about your performance!

L
is for Lateral work

In dressage, lateral movements are when your pony goes in any direction other than straight forwards. Stepping sideways in leg-yield or half-pass is lateral work, and it can also refer to shoulder-in and even rein back. Any rider and pony can try basic lateral work, and it's great to do because it'll help him become lovely and supple!

M
is for Medium trot

Did you know that as you move through the levels in dressage, you'll be asked to perform four different types of trot? These are collected, working, medium and extended. Medium trot starts to appear in some Novice tests, and it's when you ask your pony to take longer, more powerful steps. Want to know how to ace it? Then turn to p74.

N
is for Nationals

At the end of the summer and winter dressage seasons, British Dressage (BD) holds exciting championships. There are classes for every level, so it's something any rider can aim for. If you get a chance to go along and spectate, I really recommend it. You'll learn loads about dressage and maybe get to see your fave riders in action, too!

R
is for Rhythm

You'll need to help your pony find a rhythm if you want to achieve a really good dressage score. It's when his hooves move in a regular pattern, and his strides don't get quicker or slower. It's important to get this in place during his basic training, as it'll make everything else so much easier!

S
is for Serpentine

This is where you ride three or four loops across the arena, and the shape looks a bit like a snake! You can ride serpentines while you're schooling, as it's a fun exercise that'll help improve your pony's suppleness and straightness, but they're also found in some Prelim tests. The important thing is to make sure your loops are exactly the same size and, when you cross the arena, you keep your lines super-straight.

V
is for Volte

A volte is super-small circle that's 6m, 8m or 10m in diameter, and your pony will need to be really supple to ace one. In some Grand Prix tests we're asked to ride a 10m circle to the left, then the right, in a figure-of-eight shape! It's a real challenge to change your horse's bend in the middle while making sure he stays balanced.

W
is for World Cup

The Dressage World Cup Final's held once a year, and only the very best riders take part. The world is divided into different leagues, and the top riders from each one qualify for the finals. Valegro and I won the World Cup in 2014 and 2015!

X
is for X

You may not be able to see it, but X is one of the most important letters in dressage! It marks the exact centre of the arena, and you'll need to ride right over it to ace centre lines, diagonal lines, changes of rein and 20m circles.

O
is for Online dressage

You don't have to travel to a show to try dressage, as there are online comps you can enter! All you need to do is get someone to film you riding, then send the video in for judging. Not only is it great fun, it can be a great way to compete if you get nervous, because you'll feel more relaxed riding at home.

P
is for Piaffe

Dressage fans love watching a horse piaffe, which is when he trots on the spot and lifts each leg high in a really expressive way. It's similar to another crowd-pleaser, the passage, which is also a very collected trot but the horse keeps moving forward. Valegro was awesome at piaffe and passage and often scored 10 out of 10 for the moves! You can find out more about them on p58.

Q
is for Quality

To score great marks in dressage, your pony needs to have really good quality paces. This means when he walks, trots and canters, his movement looks free, supple and effortless – almost like he's floating! When Valegro was a young horse, Carl spotted that he had awesome paces, and he's certainly been proved right!

T
is for Team dressage

I love competing on teams! It's when three or four riders all perform a test, and their total score decides who wins. You don't have to be a top rider to be on a team, so look out for opportunities through your Pony Club, Riding Club or BD Quest!

U
is for Unaffiliated

This is the type of competition you can enter if you're not a member of BD. It's a great place to start if you're new to dressage, and you're sure to find there are lots of unaffiliated shows taking place at your local venues. You can still try tests at different levels and there are championships to aim for, too.

Y
is for Young horses

BD runs special classes – and championships – for young horses aged 4–7, and ponies aged 4–6. The tests are all about building confidence and supporting their training at home. Watching a young horse class is the perfect place to spot the dressage stars of the future, and it's where Valegro started his road to dressage glory!

Z
is for Zig-zag

If you want to impress your friends, try riding a zig-zag! You can do this in leg-yield by asking your pony to step to the right for a few strides, then to the left... and repeat! In Grand Prix Freestyle classes, competitors will often try and wow the judges by including a zig-zag in canter half-pass. It's a move that really does look amazing.

LIVING MY BEST LIFE

All about my life with horses

Want to find out what being a top dressage rider involves? Here are some of the awesome things I get up to – it really is the best job in the world!

An early start
I usually ride 10 horses every day, and will be on the first one by 7.45am. How long each horse is schooled for depends on what level he's at. My Advanced horses are worked for around 45mins, while the youngsters will have a shorter session of 30mins, where I'll focus on building their strength.

Luckily, I have help to warm-up and cool down the horses. One of our riders will walk them for 20mins before I get on. Then, when I've finished the schooling sesh, they'll take them for a short, relaxing hack.

Competition time
Shows take up a lot of time during the dressage season, and we'll usually be away competing at least once a week. Not all shows take place on home ground and we'll head overseas to an international event once a month.

Live events
Our fans love finding out all about how Carl and I train our horses, so we try to hold a few demos every year. As well as showing off the star horses, we'll take along our youngsters, too, because it's great experience for them.

Some of the demos take place at the yard, but we also perform them at big venues around the country. I'm often invited to give demos around the world, too, which is a huge honour.

Model behaviour
I couldn't do without the support of my lovely sponsors, and in return I offer up my time to help them. This could involve attending events, and I'm also asked to model clothing and riding kit for catalogues or ad campaigns. It's loads of fun, and I love being one of the first people to see all the new gear. My gorgeous horses make perfect models, too!

Keeping fit
You might think that schooling 10 different horses a day keeps me fit, but I also do a lot of exercise to make sure my body stays strong and supple for riding. Everything's focused on maintaining my core strength, which is so important for dressage. I have a session with a personal trainer twice a week, and I'll work out by myself at least two more times. I find spinning really useful and I've invested in my own indoor bicycle.

Riding can take a toll on my muscles, so to help keep me in tip-top condition – and sort out any aches and pains – I see a physio every two weeks. Physio's a really important part of my horses' routine as well, and they all have regular treatments.

My best-ever DRESSAGE TIPS

Unlock the secrets to being a gold medal winner!

1. Focus on the basics

If you want to be successful in dressage, the most important thing to do is ensure all the basics are firmly in place. Making sure your pony's supple, balanced, straight and responsive should be the focus of everything you do with him. Some riders race ahead because they want to try the fancy moves, but you wouldn't build a house without laying strong foundations, and the same goes for your pony's training.

2. Watch and learn

When I was starting out in dressage, I'd watch other riders, and I learned so much from them. It can actually be more helpful than having a lesson. You might not always understand what your instructor's asking you to do, but if you watch someone perform a movement correctly, you can see exactly where you need to place your leg or position your body.

3. Set yourself goals

Stay motivated by setting goals and giving yourself something to work towards. You could aim high and focus on winning an Olympic medal, but even learning a new movement or improving your dressage percentage at a certain level can inspire you to work harder and keep polishing your performance.

4. Ditch the nerves

Don't let being nervous take the fun out of competing. My tip is to imagine you're not at a show but riding in the arena at home – it really works for me! You'll feel way more relaxed, so you can enjoy yourself and it'll make it easier for you to remember your test, too!

5. Know your pony

Try to feel and understand how your pony moves and thinks, rather than just steering him from letter to letter. Consider the way he responds to your aids, and how you could improve the communication between you. Another thing to think about is what works best when you're teaching him something new. If he gets bored easily, for example, introduce some polework to help keep him interested.

6. Develop balance and feel

My riding position is strong and secure because of all the lessons I've had on the lunge, and I really recommend you book some, too. Taking away your reins and stirrups while your instructor controls your pony is super-useful. It'll help you develop an independent seat, good balance and feel, which are all so important for dressage.

7. Be prepared

It's not just how you ride each movement in a test, it's how you prepare for them that'll get you extra marks. Use the corners to set your pony up for what's coming next, and learn how to ride half-halts. This is when you ask your pony to wait for just a moment, then ride him forward again, which helps to keep him balanced. I ride loads in all of my tests – why not ask your instructor to show you how?

8. Shorten your reins

I'm sure you've heard me say that short reins win gold medals, and it's true! It's the best way to make sure your hands are going towards your pony's mouth, which creates a better connection through your reins, and is much more pleasant for him. If you ride with long reins there's a good chance you'll pull your hands back towards your body, which tells your pony to stop, not go!

Make VALEGRO COOKIES

These tasty biscuits look just like dressage star Valegro

To make the shortbread

1. Place the butter and caster sugar in your mixing bowl and beat until it's just soft.
2. Add the egg yolk and flour and mix together until you've got a stiff dough.
3. Roll the dough into a ball, then remove it from the bowl, wrap it in cling film and pop it in the fridge to chill for approx one hour.
4. Preheat the oven to 200°c (180°c if you've got a fan oven) or gas mark 6, and line your baking trays with non-stick paper.
5. Remove the dough from the fridge and roll it out on a slightly floured surface. Aim for the thickness of a £1 coin, which is approx 3mm.
6. Using the Valegro template and a sharp knife (ask an adult to help you with this), cut out the biscuits. Carefully place them onto your baking trays.
7. Bake the cookies for 10-15 mins until they're a light golden colour. Leave them on the baking trays to cool, to avoid breaking them.

To create the decoration

1. Dust your work surface with icing sugar, then take the rolling pin and roll out the brown sugar paste until it's about half the thickness of the biscuits.
2. Cut out Valegro shapes from the sugar paste – you'll need your template for this.
3. Carefully lay the sugar paste cut-outs onto each biscuit, and smooth them on gently with your fingers. Allow to set.
4. Make the cookies look even more like Valegro with the writing icing! You'll need black for his mane and features, brown for outlining his head and white for colouring in his blaze. You can also use a fine paintbrush and a little brown food colouring to paint in more detail if you like.

WHAT YOU'LL NEED

Shortbread biscuits:
- 200g salted butter (softened)
- 100g caster sugar
- 1 medium-sized egg yolk
- 260g plain flour, plus a little extra for rolling out

Icing
- dark brown sugar paste
- brown, black and white writing icing
- icing sugar to dust

Tools
- mixing bowl
- wooden spoon
- rolling pin
- Valegro template – you'll find this on p85
- two baking trays
- greaseproof/non-stick baking paper
- cling film
- sharp knife
- wire cooling rack

" Valegro thinks these super-cute cookies look really tasty! **"**

top tip
If the sugar paste cracks while you're decorating the biscuits, gently rub it to smooth it out.

SUPER CIRCLES

Ace these school shapes and score higher marks

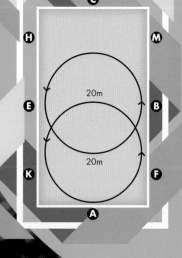

You might think riding a large circle is super-simple, but it's actually trickier than it sounds. Many riders struggle to make them the right shape and size, and dressage judges probably see a lot more ovals and squares than perfectly round circles! They're worth practising, though, because a well-ridden circle will earn you easy marks in a test. Here's how...

HOW TO RIDE IT

1. If you're riding a 20m circle from A or C, ask your pony for a little inside bend just before you reach the letter. This will make sure you start the circle exactly when his shoulders are level with the marker. To achieve the perfect bend in his body, flex his head and neck slightly to the inside by opening your inside rein and hold the outside rein against his withers. Press your inside leg on the girth to encourage him to bend around it, and place your outside leg just behind the girth to make sure his hindquarters don't swing out.
2. To help guide your pony, turn your head, shoulders and torso to follow the curve of the circle. Keep looking up in the direction you want to go.
3. Aim to touch the track at a point that's 10m away from the short side.
4. Circle away from the track and ride all the way to X, before briefly returning to the track on the opposite side and finishing the circle back at A or C.
5. Now try riding a 20m circle in the middle of the arena from E or B, which is a little bit trickier. This time your circle will pass through two invisible points that are 10m either side of X. To help you get the shape spot-on you can measure out the distance and place markers there to ride through. Then have a go without them and see how accurate you are!

top tip

I always imagine the outline of the circle, then follow that line with my horse's shoulders. Another hint is to pretend you're riding a diamond shape, which helps you touch the track in the right places!

FINE-TUNE YOUR FLATWORK

Fault: My circles are square, not round!
Fix it: This is easily sorted by remembering that circles don't have corners! Instead of riding right into each corner, follow a curved line that goes approx 1m inside it. Also, keep your outside leg behind the girth so you can correct your pony quickly if he starts to drift out beyond the shape you're aiming for.

Fault: My pony's head curls to the inside of the circle and his quarters swing to the outside.
Fix it: You're creating too much bend in your pony's body. You only need a little flexion, so he has a soft curve from nose to tail – if you have the perfect amount you'll just be able to see the corner of his inside eye!

DID YOU KNOW?

As well as riding a perfectly round and correctly-sized shape, the judge will want to see your pony stay in an even rhythm with good impulsion all the way around the circle.

Fabulous

FREESTYLE

Mount St John Freestyle oozes talent – it's why she's known as Mrs Valegro! Read on to find out more about her

FACT FILE
Name: Mount St John Freestyle
Stable name: Mrs Valegro
Foaled: 2009
Colour: Bay
Breed: Hanoverian, by Fidermark
Height: 16.3hh
Owned by: Mount St John Stud
Fast fact: Freestyle loves her work and really enjoys competing, too.

Mount St John Freestyle, with her dazzlingly good looks and trademark floppy ears, is a firm favourite on our yard – could she be any cuter? I've been riding Freestyle, as she's known on the yard, for six years, since she was just five years old. Since then, she's proved that she's got limitless ability and has clocked up loads of wins, and I really think the sky's the limit for this uber-talented mare.

Home from home
Born in Germany in May 2009, Freestyle was bought from the Elite Hanoverian foal auction in Verden by Mount St John Stud. The stud's based in North Yorkshire, and is run and owned by Emma Blundell.

Freestyle immediately caught Emma's eye, and was actually the first foal bought by the stud! Emma was in charge of all Freestyle's early training, and they qualified to compete at the British Dressage National Championships together. They came an amazing sixth in the four-year-old finals! Emma was blown away by Freestyle's talent and I was really excited when she asked me to compete her – I couldn't wait to have a sit on this special horse.

When I met Freestyle, her huge eyes and floppy ears were the first things that caught my eye. Also, her looks, the way she moved and her personality really reminded me of Valegro's wow-factor, so I definitely felt the potential for a great partnership. Thankfully, she's proved me right and is such an amazing horse to train and compete.

DID YOU KNOW?
When we won our first Grand Prix Special, I hadn't even practised the test with her!

DID YOU KNOW?
In our first ever competition together, Freestyle and I won a Medium test with a score of 78%.

27

ROLL OF HONOUR

- 1st, Hickstead Rotterdam Grand Prix Challenge 2020

- 1st, Grand Prix Freestyle, Olympia 2019

- 4th (team), Continental Championships 2019, Rotterdam

- Individual bronze, World Equestrian Games 2018 Tryon, USA

- Team bronze, World Equestrian Games 2018

- 1st, Windsor Horse Show 2018 Grand Prix and Grand Prix Freestyle to Music

Big on personality

I'm sure everyone knows a mare who's a larger-than-life character, and Freestyle certainly fits that description! While she may not be mareish, and she's certainly never naughty, she does have the occasional cheeky moment. She's as good as gold when we're training at home, but will often call out for her friends when we're away at shows.

She's not a spooky horse, but she does look to me for a little confidence boost when we're competing in an indoor arena. With a bigger atmosphere, plenty of noise and crowds virtually on top of you, it takes some bravery to perform at your best indoors. However, the more big shows we've done, the happier she's become.

Freestyle is super-cuddly, too, which makes her a firm favourite on the yard. She loves everyone and is very affectionate.

DID YOU KNOW?

Foals bred by Mount St John stud have the prefix MSJ, while horses bought by the stud have Mount St John in full.

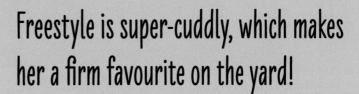

> # Freestyle is super-cuddly, which makes her a firm favourite on the yard!

Party trick

Never one to let down the crowds, Freestyle absolutely loves prize-givings! She always gives a cheeky wave of her foreleg to her adoring fans when we collect our prizes. Once, at Royal Windsor Horse Show, she even gave the Royal Box a double wave, much to the shock of the judges! I didn't quite expect a cheeky rear – perhaps she was showing off for the Queen!

The next generation

Mount St John Freestyle doesn't spend all her time showing off in the dressage ring – she's also a grandmother! Alongside her spectacular competition record, she's produced three foals via embryo transfer – this means the foals are genetically hers, but they were carried and given birth to by a surrogate mare, allowing Freestyle to carry on training and competing.

Her foals, MSJ A La Freestyle, MSJ Dancefloor and MSJ Streetdance are showing plenty of promise in the dressage arena, too, and one of her offspring has gone on to have her a foal of her own.

Pony swaps

She may be my number one girl, but Freestyle sometimes enjoys a schooling session with Carl! A little variety is a great way to spice up the horses' routines, and it's useful to get help from such an awesome rider. Carl and I often swap rides at home so we can watch our own horses in action. You'll spot things that you can't feel in the saddle and, just like looking back at a video of yourself schooling or competing, it can be invaluable to your training.

YARD tour

Go behind-the-scenes at the stables

Oaklebrook Mill is one of the most famous yards in the whole world, and it really is an amazing place. I'm so lucky to be able to work here and keep my horses here. To show you just how very special it is, let me take you on a tour behind the scenes...

Picture perfect
Visitors approach Oaklebrook Mill down a long, sweeping driveway. It's a taste of things to come as it's very picturesque and there's not a blade of grass out of place! When they reach the gate to the yard, the first thing they'll see is this amazing life-size sculpture of a dancing horse!

A stable life
At such a busy yard there's always something going on, but we try really hard to keep the stables area calm and peaceful, so the horses can relax when they're inside. Each stable has an extra window, which makes them light and airy, and the horses can enjoy a change of view. There are also grilles between each stable, so they can interact with each other when they're inside, too.

We always tack up and wash the horses off after exercise in a special area at one end of the indoor school, next to the tack room. This means that all their work-related stuff is separate from where they chill out, and we think that's much healthier for them.

DID YOU KNOW?
The front of the stables are made from bricks that came from an old hospital!

DID YOU KNOW?
There are 18 boxes on the main yard, plus our Olympic superstars, Valegro and Uthopia, have their own stables at the yard entrance!

School's out – or in!
We're very lucky that we have an indoor school to ride in, so we can exercise the horses whatever the weather. It's enormous, and is one of the nicest indoor arenas I've ever been in! It's very light, because it's open along one side, and there are loads of mirrors so we can keep an eye on what our horses are doing – and our riding position, of course!

Our outdoor arena's 60x20m, and it's where we practise our tests for all the big competitions. It's surrounded by a smart box hedge, and is very beautiful. It has a raised area at one end so Carl can teach in comfort. Even the arena letters are works of art!

Birds in paradise

It's not just horses that are a big part of life at the yard, there are usually a few dogs around, too. Plus, Carl has many feathered friends in the form of peacocks, guinea fowl and chickens. They have free rein to go wherever they like, and will often wander into the school when you're riding! It's actually very good for teaching the horses to cope with anything and everything, and means that all the sights and sounds of a competition don't really bother them.

DID YOU KNOW?
We often hold tours, so you could come and see for yourself how amazing the yard is!

Dance WITH ME

Find out all about dressage to music

I absolutely love dressage to music because it's so much fun. As well as getting to dance with your pony, you create the test yourself and use it to show off all his best moves! Everyone can try it, too, as there are competitions from Prelim all the way through to Grand Prix. Fancy having a go? Here are my tips to help you put together a winning performance!

All the right moves

When you enter a dressage to music class, you get to choreograph the test yourself! This is called creating a floorplan and you'll be able to include lots of moves that your pony's good at, plus there'll be a few compulsory ones to add in, too. Don't forget, though, that the moves need to be relevant for your level of competition, so don't get too carried away!

top tip

Your dressage to music test should be symmetrical, so remember to ride all of the movements on both reins.

Face the music

When you select the music you'll perform your test to, pick tunes that make you feel excited and positive about performing. I know when my music's just right because it gives me goosebumps! I'm lucky that I've got an amazing composer, Tom Hunt, to help me, and we work together to make sure my music perfectly matches my floorplan. You can still get great results doing it all yourself, though, and choosing music that suits your pony's type and personality is a great place to start. Because Valegro's strong and powerful, the *How to Train Your Dragon* soundtrack suited him really well. In contrast, Freestyle's very ballerina like, so the music from *Frozen* was a much better match.

While some ponies love music and will perform even better to it than in a normal test, it can make others hot and tense. If your pony's nervous, soft, quiet music that doesn't have any crashing and banging will help keep him calm. If he's really laid-back, use something dramatic to help you add a little more sparkle to his paces.

Feel the rhythm

It's really important that your music matches your pony's paces. You want him to step along to the beat, as this will look really impressive! This means you'll need to select different music for his walk, trot and canter. To work this out, ask someone to film you riding in all of the paces, then watch the video back while listening to different tunes. You'll soon be able to spot what fits and what doesn't.

DID YOU KNOW?

You'll have a time limit for your test, so make sure it's the correct length.

On your marks

In dressage to music you'll be scored for each move, like in a normal test, and you'll also be given artistic marks for your overall performance. Here the judge will be looking to reward you for how well you interpreted your music, and how your pony flows from one move to the next. There are also marks for how well you use the space in the arena, and the partnership you have with your pony.

Tips from the top

Valegro and I have ridden some awesome Freestyle tests together. Here's how you can make sure you always give your performances the wow factor...

- **stand out from the crowd** Aim to choose music that's not often used by other riders. Judges get bored of hearing the same songs over and over again!

- **get some inspo** There's loads of amazing tests online that you can watch, and they'll give you some brilliant ideas to try out yourself

- **be creative** I like to use my floorplan and music to tell a story. An easy way to do this is to ride transitions and begin movements at the same time as changes happen in the music

STAR POTENTIAL

How to spot a future dressage champion

There's so much to think about when looking for a new horse, and while talent is a must for a future dressage star, temperament and trainability are super-important, too. Here are a few of the things that will be on my list...

Perfect paces
A young horse can tell me so much by the way he moves, even if he hasn't had any dressage training yet. I want to see that he has three good paces that I can make amazing! I might actually be put off by youngsters who have a huge, extravagant trot and canter, because they can be harder to train and could be more prone to injury.

Looks
It's hard to resist a stunning horse! However, while good looks will catch my eye, they aren't vital in a youngster. It's a bonus, but even a plain horse will look really special when he's been trained to move beautifully.

Trainability
A horse may have talent, but it's no good if he doesn't want to work with you. I need a horse who's willing and honest, and always tries his best for me. Of course, you might not find this out until you get him home and training begins, but I'll look for subtle clues when I'm trying out a horse. I want him to be alert and interested, and have a positive attitude.

Conformation
A dressage horse needs to be 'uphill', which means his neck is higher than his quarters. This'll make it easier for him to carry himself and his rider in good balance. I'm also a fan of horses who are strong and built to last. I love the old-fashioned type like Valegro. He has a leg in each corner and is a bit chunkier than a lot of today's dressage horses, who are more finely built.

I think my homebred, Mowgli, is going to be a superstar

Temperament

This goes hand-in-hand with trainability, and a horse who's calm, friendly and well-behaved is so much nicer to be around, plus they'll probably be easier to work with, too.

A kind eye

I always look at a horse's eye when I'm considering buying him. I like a big eye, but not a really round eye. It's a personal preference, but I wouldn't buy a horse with a white eye.

Better bred

While I can try to buy a future Olympic champion, my other option is to breed one! I'm lucky that I have incredibly talented mares like Freestyle and Flora to help me produce a star of the future.

I may be biased but I think my youngster Limited Edition (Mowgli) – who's pictured here – is pretty much the perfect horse! For a start, his family tree couldn't be any more impressive. Mowgli's mum is my gorgeous mare Flora, and his dad is the famous dressage stallion Negro. This makes Mowgli Valegro's half brother!

The Valegro connection isn't the only reason that I chose Negro. I carefully considered the positive things Flora could pass on to her foal, and what may be missing. I decided I'd like to add some strength to her build, so Negro seemed the right choice.

Mowgli's now aged four and has grown into a lovely horse. As well as looking amazing, he has an incredible temperament.

Just like with his mum, I'm taking his training slowly and he's spent more time hacking than schooling. This is because he's a big horse and I want to work on strengthening his muscles. Hopefully he'll do a few Novice tests soon, and I'll also try to take him to some demos, which are great for teaching young horses to cope with crowds and lots of atmosphere.

DID YOU KNOW?

Mowgli's show name is Limited Edition because I've decided he's the only foal Flora will have!

KEEPING MY
horses happy

Happy horses who love their life will give you so much more in the competition arena

The horses Carl and I train have a busy schedule which, of course, includes regular training to keep them on top form and prepared for the demands of competition. But it's not all dancing in the arena – far from it, actually! If our horses did the same thing day-in, day-out and tackled the most difficult dressage movements all the time, they wouldn't be quite as enthusiastic about their work as they are. Keeping the horses in a routine they thrive on is a delicate balance, but I think we've found the recipe for success that helps them stay happy and healthy.

Hacks galore!
We don't spend all our time in the school, and hacking's an important part of the horses' training regime. Not only is it amazing for cardiovascular fitness – in other words, helping them get used to working harder for longer – it's a great way to keep them interested and gives them plenty of sights and sounds to enjoy. They sometimes even go for a quick warm-up hack before a schooling session, so they head into the arena fresh and happy. You can discover more of my hacking tips on p70!

DID YOU KNOW?
Even though they are dressage horses, I'm not against them trying new things. They might even pop over a little jump every once in a while!

Spa day
We're lucky to have amazing facilities at our yard, all of which play a big role in keeping our horses relaxed and allowing them to perform to their best. Regular sessions in the solarium – where they stand under heat lamps – help warm their muscles up before they're ridden, and it's a handy place to dry them off after a bath.

My horses enjoy weekly physiotherapy or massage sessions, too, which help keep them in tip-top shape, and eases any tightness that may have developed in their muscles. In between treatments, I'll pop a massage pad on them.

In the saddle
If every training session involved high-level movements, my horses would get bored and it would be really hard work for them. My philosophy is less is more, and I don't train the top-level stuff all the time – I rarely ride through full dressage tests, either. If you train the complex stuff well, and the horses are confident and secure in what they're doing, they'll remember the difficult movements and you won't need to run through them too often.

Making a splash

I'm always looking for ways to boost my horses' strength and fitness, and I'm a big fan of the aqua walker. It's a treadmill that's under water and looks like a giant bath! Walking the horses through the water gives their legs a gentle, low-impact workout and it adds even more variety to their schedule.

Turnout time

You might think that much of a competition horse's life is spent in the stable, but our horses enjoy going out in the field every day. It's so good for their minds and bodies to be outside, moving and grazing and just being a horse. If we're not at a show, they have Sundays off – you wouldn't want to go to school every day of the week, and neither do they!

DID YOU KNOW?

I'll often pop the horses on the walker to break up the time they spend in the stable – they really appreciate having an extra leg stretch.

Reap the rewards

One of the keys to having a happy horse is letting him know when he's done well. I reward all my horses' good work, and let them have a stretch and a breather when they've tried hard for me. I'll give them lots of walk breaks within a session so they can chill out, and then they feel refreshed and enthusiastic when I pick up the reins to move on to the next exercise.

Simple rules

My tried-and-tested management routine ensures my horses have variety, plenty of rest and reward, and lots of fun, too! But most of all, I'm always thinking about new things I can do to make their lifestyle suit them even better. Maybe your pony could benefit from a management shake-up? Get creative and see what he responds to – you might find he loves to warm up for schooling with a hack, or a few hours of extra turnout makes him more chilled to ride. A happy horse performs better, and you might notice an increase in his enthusiasm levels all-round.

RIDE THE PERFECT CENTRE LINE

Make an entrance that'll wow the judge every time

Starting your dressage test with an epic straight line won't just score you a high mark, it'll give you a confidence boost that'll help you ride brilliantly all the way through to your final halt. Here's how to wow the judge in every test you ride...

top tip
To make a smoother turn at A, it can help to imagine you're riding a half 10m circle from F or K to D.

HOW TO RIDE IT

1. Start your preparation for the centre line well before you enter at A. So, while you're riding around the edge of the arena waiting for the bell to ring, make sure your pony's going forward in an active trot.
2. Approach from the long side and, as you come out of the corner before A, look up and ahead to where you want to go. When you turn, guide your pony by opening your inside rein a little and pressing your inside leg on the girth. At the same time, place your outside rein against his wither to allow him to bend, while keeping a steady contact with his mouth. Your outside leg goes just behind the girth to stop his quarters from drifting out.
3. When you're on the centre line, fix your eyes on the judge at C and ride straight towards them. You can widen your hands a little to help channel your pony along the line you want, and wrap your legs around his sides to keep a lovely, energetic trot. Don't forget to smile, too!
4. Complete your perfect centre line with a smooth turn at C. A few strides away from the letter, look up and ahead to where you want to go, which will let your pony know which direction you'll be turning.

CHARLOTTE DUJARDIN

A great centre line starts with a smooth turn at A

top tip

Try turning a little earlier onto the centre line than you think, so you don't overshoot it. Imagine there's a wall at A, and you need to ride just inside it!

FINE-TUNE YOUR FLATWORK

Fault: My pony curls to the inside when I turn at A, so our centre line's always crooked.
Fix it: Remember to guide your pony around the turn by using your outside leg and rein. Don't try to just pull him round with your inside rein, because this will make him curl up.

Fault: My pony tips onto his forehand as we make our turn at A and loses impulsion, which makes him extra wobbly.
Fix it: It's really important that your pony's carrying himself in good balance and isn't relying on you to hold him together with your rein contact. To solve this you'll need to work on exercises that make him more supple, such as serpentines, and ones that encourage him to push more from behind, such as riding lots of transitions.

Check it out

You can check your pony's moving in self-carriage by giving and retaking your rein contact. Push your reins forward up his neck, count to three, then gradually take the contact back again. Your pony should stay in the same outline. If he falls onto his forehand it's because you've been holding him up with your reins.

39

Gorgeous GIO

Get to know my small but powerful horse Gio

I fell in love with Gio – aka Pumpkin – the very first time I set eyes on him. It was at a clinic I was giving in America, and he caught my attention straight away. He came into the arena with his ears pricked and such a cute expression on his face, and I just wanted to know what he was like to ride!

DID YOU KNOW?
Gio was given the stable name Pumpkin because he arrived on Halloween!

Star spotting

Pumpkin was five years old when his then owner, Amelie Kovac, brought him along to my clinic in California. They could only come because someone else dropped out last minute, so it feels like fate played a hand in bringing us together!

He was on the small side for a dressage horse, but I could tell this handsome chestnut gelding was something special, and I asked Amelie if she'd let me ride him in a demo the following day. She was thrilled and said yes.

At the demo, Pumpkin proved to be a dream to ride, and I was really impressed how he coped with being in front of a big crowd, too. I decided I wanted to buy this very exciting young horse, but knew I'd have to act quickly before anyone else spotted his star potential! Luckily, I managed to persuade Amelie to part with him. She loved Pumpkin a lot, and it was a difficult decision for her, but she agreed because I wanted to keep and ride him myself. One month later, in October 2015, Pumpkin arrived at our yard in Gloucestershire!

A successful debut

I brought Pumpkin on slowly and it was over a year before we did our first competition together. Luckily it was a successful day and in February 2017 we won two Elementary tests!

From there, he has gone from strength to strength and is now successfully competing at Grand Prix. He's such a nice horse with a big heart and he loves cuddles! He may be small in size, but he's definitely not short on character!

DID YOU KNOW?
I was only the second person ever to sit on Pumpkin!

DID YOU KNOW?
Because Pumpkin's quite small, Carl said he thought I'd bought a pony!

DID YOU KNOW?
Pumpkin scored a massive 79.5% in his first ever Grand Prix.

ROLL OF HONOUR

- 1st, Grand Prix, Addington High Profile Show 2020

- 1st, Inter II, British Dressage National Champs 2019

- 1st, Inter II, Hartpury Premier League 2019

- 2nd, Advanced Medium, British Dressage National Champs 2018

- 1st, Advanced Medium, Hartpury Premier League 2018

Q&A

I'M HAPPIEST WHEN...

Find out loads more about me by checking out this fun Q&A

I'm happiest when...
I'm riding. Doing what I love makes me happy, and horses are my passion.

If I wasn't a professional rider, I'd have loved to...
work for an equine charity or be a vet nurse. It would definitely have been something involving animals.

My most treasured possession
my horses. They mean the world to me.

To relax I enjoy...
walking my dogs, or spending time with my family.

My least favourite yard chore is...
sweeping up. It's just not a job I enjoy.

On a Friday night you can find me...
out with friends. We'd either go for a meal – I love food – or head to the cinema to watch a film.

If I want to treat myself...
I'll buy some shoes, sunglasses or a handbag. I'm a big fan of shopping!

The person I most admire is...
Serena Williams, who's won Wimbledon seven times. She's an incredible person who has achieved so much and I admire her determination and willpower.

My favourite journey is...
travelling to New Zealand. I love the flight because all I have to do is eat and sleep, and when you arrive it's the most incredible country. Pumpkins' part-owner, Renai Hart, lives there and I usually visit for one month each year. I'll fit in some teaching, so it's not just a holiday!

Growing up my hero was... Carl Hester, of course!

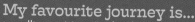

My lucky mascots are... two special teddies. One was given to me by the girls at the yard and is called Delilah. The other's a horse called Norman who was the mascot for the World Equestrian Games in 2014, where we won two individual gold medals and team silver. I always keep the mascots I'm given at events.

The show I most love competing at is...
Olympia. It's awesome to be competing on home ground, it's Christmassy and the atmosphere is electric. I also love that I get to go shopping in London!

POSITION PERFECT

How to ride like an Olympic champion!

Your riding position is really important for dressage success. When you sit correctly in the saddle you'll be in perfect harmony with your pony, and will be able to communicate effortlessly with him through your rein, leg and seat aids. But, if you're crooked or tipping forward or back, you'll put him off balance, which means he won't be able to stay straight and he'll struggle to carry himself and perform all the movements properly. Here's what you need to know to adopt that perfect position...

Hands

Loads of riders tilt their hands like they're pushing a shopping trolley, but it's super-important to imagine you're carrying a tray of drinks instead! This'll encourage you to keep your thumbs on top of the reins and wrists soft, which all helps create a light, elastic contact with your pony's mouth.

Legs

Softly hug your pony's sides with your legs, but keep your thighs and knees relaxed so they're not gripping the saddle. Your lower leg must stay still, and not swing backwards or forwards, to help you stay in balance and so you can give your pony precise aids.

Head

Your head's one of the heaviest part of your body, so if you look down it'll put more of your weight over your pony's shoulders, making it harder for him to stay in balance. It's really important to always look ahead to help keep your head in the right place.

Shoulders

Relax your shoulders and roll them back to help you sit up straight. When you're in a correct riding position you should be able to draw a straight line that runs from your ear to your shoulder and hip, all the way down to your heel.

Elbows

The contact you have on your pony's mouth should be soft and allowing, and this all comes from your elbows! Remember to have a slight bend in them, and keep them tucked in against your sides. If your arms are straight, you won't be able to stay soft in your forearms and your rein contact won't feel as secure.

Seat

Your seat helps you communicate with your horse or pony. To be able to use it effectively, make sure you sit centrally, in the deepest part of the saddle, and have your weight evenly distributed over both seat bones.

Feet

The ball of your foot should rest on the stirrup iron, with your toes facing forward and upwards. Lift your toes up, so they're slightly higher than your heels.

Make
A ROSETTE DISPLAY

An epic way to show off all your hard-earned rosettes

WHAT YOU'LL NEED
- large picture frame, with the centre removed
- wood paint (optional)
- wide ribbon or bias binding tape
- staple gun
- scissors

1 If you want to change the colour of your picture frame, paint it and leave to dry.

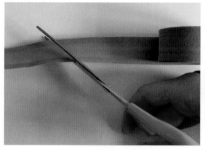

2 Cut your ribbon or tape into strips that are long enough to go diagonally from one side of the frame to the other.

top tip

Always ask an adult for help when using a staple gun.

3 Take the first strip and place it diagonally across the frame. Secure in place on both sides using a staple gun, keeping the ribbon or tape taught.

4 Repeat with the other pieces of ribbon/tape, leaving approx 2-3cm between each one.

5 Now do the same in the other direction, but weave each strip of ribbon in and out, to create a criss-cross pattern.

6 Hang up your frame, then hook or pin your rosettes onto the ribbon. Ta-dah!

top tip

You can pin photos of your fave pony around the frame, or personalise it by painting on his name!

Get to know me

Check out these nine amazing facts

DID YOU KNOW?
When I needed to improve my core strength to ace sitting trot, I swam 50-70 lengths every morning before heading down to the stables.

DID YOU KNOW?
Having won three gold and one silver medal, I'm Great Britain's most successful Olympic equestrian.

DID YOU KNOW?
I first went to Carl Hester's yard as a temporary groom, then never left!

DID YOU KNOW?
I made a guest appearance in the horsey TV show Free Rein – and got to meet Bob, Raven, Elvis and Firefly!

DID YOU KNOW?
There are some houses named after me in my home town of Enfield, and who wouldn't want to live in Valegro Avenue, which is close to our stables in Gloucestershire?

DID YOU KNOW?
Valegro and I hold the world records for achieving the highest scores ever in all three Grand Prix tests.

" I always help with the mucking out on Christmas day "

DID YOU KNOW?
When I wanted to teach my first horse to piaffe, I bought a Carl Hester DVD to show me how.

DID YOU KNOW?
I started a new trend in Grand Prix dressage when, following a nasty fall, I started wearing a helmet with a chinstrap instead of a top hat for competitions. Now loads of people wear the same.

DID YOU KNOW?
I always help with the mucking out on Christmas day! It's actually one of my favourite yard chores!

7 REASONS DRESSAGE IS THE BEST

Why you should make this your new favourite discipline

1. It's for everyone

One of the best things about dressage is that anyone can have a go! In Intro tests you only have to walk and trot, so you can ease yourself into test riding gently. Then, if you want to progress from there you can try a Prelim test that has some simple canter work. Maybe you'll be bitten by the dressage bug and want to move up to Novice and beyond? With the right training for you and your pony, the sky's the limit!

2. You'll get schooling inspo

Working towards a dressage test will help you really focus your fave pony's schooling sessions. You can divide the test up into bite-sized chunks at first and practise some of the trickier moves over a number of days until you get them spot-on. It's good to research some useful exercises that'll help you improve, too, so you can perform your test like a pro!

3. You can create a great partnership

To ace all the moves in a dressage test you and your fave pony need to work as a team. Your job's to work out what instructions you need to give him to correctly navigate all the moves in a test. He must listen to you and react as soon as you ask. Being able to tune into each other like this will turn you into perfect partners in no time!

top tip

Why not ask someone to video you while you ride your test? It's another fab way to track your progress, as you can watch it back whenever you like!

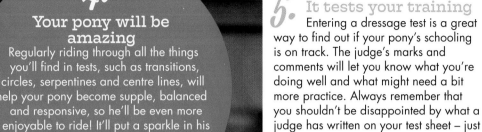

4. Your pony will be amazing

Regularly riding through all the things you'll find in tests, such as transitions, circles, serpentines and centre lines, will help your pony become supple, balanced and responsive, so he'll be even more enjoyable to ride! It'll put a sparkle in his paces and help him perform better in other areas of his ridden work, too, including hacking and jumping.

5. It tests your training

Entering a dressage test is a great way to find out if your pony's schooling is on track. The judge's marks and comments will let you know what you're doing well and what might need a bit more practice. Always remember that you shouldn't be disappointed by what a judge has written on your test sheet – just see their comments as useful feedback that'll help you be even more brilliant at your next show!

6. You can track your progress

Keep all your test sheets somewhere safe and, after you've done a few competitions, take a look back through them. They're a really useful way to see how you and your pony are progressing. Hopefully, your scores will be going in the right direction, but if not you can use the sheets to remind you of the areas you should be focusing on.

7. You'll embrace new challenges

As you ride different tests and move up through the levels, there'll be something new for you and your pony to learn. This is brilliant because you'll always have a goal to aim for, which will help you stay motivated and keep your pony's schooling on track. Plus, it's an amazing feeling when you've mastered a new move.

MAKING Memories

Take a look inside my photo album

Olympic Champion 2012 – the smile on my face says it all!

I was alway[s] destined to [be] a rider.

I adore my dogs as much as I love my horses.

This Valegro look-a-like hob[by] horse is just adorable!

The stable yard – one of my favourite places.

Celebrating a win at Windsor with Freestyle.

Carl and I behind the scenes at the Rio 2016 Olympics.

Blueberry took everything in his stride when he met the Queen at Windsor Horse Show.

I love this perfect pose of my pets.

Valegro's retirement ceremony was such an emotional moment.

Our retirement village! Blueberry and Carl's former Olympic ride Uthopia have their own private stable block.

WHAT KIND OF
COMPETITOR ARE YOU?

Are you a mega-competitive rider, or the most chilled out competitor ever? Find out with my super-fun quiz...

On time is fine

How often are you likely to practise?

Not too much, I don't want to overdo it

Loads, I have to get it right

Do you often leave things to the last minute?

No

Checking I have everything

Yes

How would you describe your warm-up routine?

I follow a strict plan

Are you nervous about making mistakes?

Yes

Trying to settle into the vibe so my pony and I feel confident

No

GO-WITH-THE-FLOW RIDER

You're super-chilled and never let negative comments, low marks, or forgotten kit ruin your vibe! Your pony appreciates your easy-going attitude, but imagine how well you could perform with a little more organisation? Why not make a list of everything you need to take with you? You could also ask your instructor for some extra homework so you can be even more awesome in your next test!

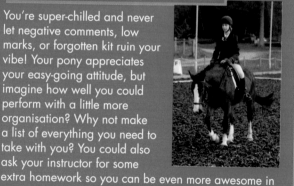

CAUTIOUS COMPETITOR

You're hardworking and always do the best you can on every ride. You try to avoid mistakes at all costs, and are likely to practise your test loads before a show. It's great to care so much about doing well, but don't let your perfectionism get in the way of enjoying yourself! If something doesn't quite go to plan, learn from the experience and use it to focus your training at home. You'll be even more brilliant next time out!

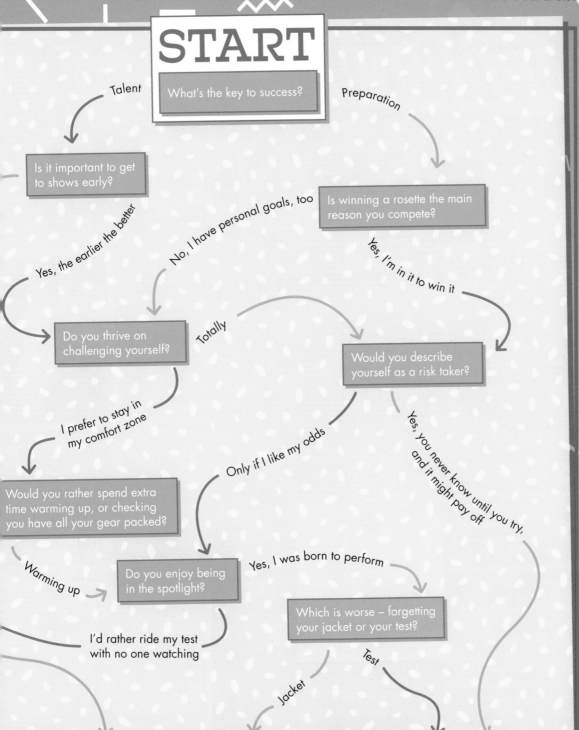

START

What's the key to success?

Talent → **Is it important to get to shows early?**

Preparation → **Is winning a rosette the main reason you compete?**

Yes, the earlier the better ↓

No, I have personal goals, too ↓

Yes, I'm in it to win it →

Do you thrive on challenging yourself?

Totally → **Would you describe yourself as a risk taker?**

I prefer to stay in my comfort zone ↓

Only if I like my odds ↓

Yes, you never know until you try, and it might pay off ↓

Would you rather spend extra time warming up, or checking you have all your gear packed?

Warming up ↓

Do you enjoy being in the spotlight?

Yes, I was born to perform →

Which is worse – forgetting your jacket or your test?

I'd rather ride my test with no one watching ↓

Jacket ↓

Test ↓

MEGA-ORGANISED COMPETITOR

You've got a training schedule, a kit list for the lorry and carefully plan your timings for every competition down to a T. You're as organised as they come and always on-the-ball – you hit every marker in a test, too. Having such brilliant attention to detail is going to make sure you go far in dressage, but don't forget to have a good time when you compete. You should have the confidence that you've dotted every i and crossed every t, so smile when you turn down the centre line and enjoy the ride!

SUPER-COMPETITIVE RIDER

You're mega-serious about dressage and always strive for the best results. You're driven, ambitious and put your all into doing well. You love performing to a crowd, too, and so does your pony! Just remember that getting a rosette's great, but dressage is all about having fun, and a ribbon's just the icing on the cake! If one comp doesn't go your way, don't focus on the negatives, but think about all the positive things from the day, including spending quality time with your pony!

Fantastic
FLORENTINA

Find out more about this gorgeous and very talented grey mare

Looks, ability and a beautiful temperament – Florentina certainly has it all! I bought this eye-catching mare from an auction when she was two years old. Her dad is Vivaldi, who's a super-popular Warmblood stallion. His offspring are usually very rideable and trainable, and Flora's certainly no exception!

Worth the wait

It's really exciting to have a very talented horse, and when I first sat on Flora I knew she was destined for great things in the dressage world. The judges love her, too, and as we've moved through the levels she's just kept winning. However, I feel that it's really important to take as much time as you need when producing horses, and I didn't compete Flora at all in 2019. This was because I wanted to focus on improving her strength and body shape before she moved up to Grand Prix level. The work I've put in has really paid off and now she looks and feels even more amazing. She's definitely ready to wow the judges at the very highest levels of dressage!

DID YOU KNOW?
Flora and I have won 31 out of the 37 classes we've competed in together.

ROLL OF HONOUR

- 1st, Inter I Freestyle to Music, Liverpool Horse Show 2018

- 1st, Inter I Freestyle to Music, Inter I and Prix St Georges, British Dressage National Championships 2018

- 1st, Inter I Freestyle to Music and Prix St Georges, Bolesworth 2018

- 1st, Inter I Freestyle to Music, Intermediate I and Prix St Georges, CDI Nieuw, Netherlands 2018

Super-sassy

Who doesn't love a horse with a big personality? Flora's such a nice mare and is very genuine – she enjoys her work and always tries her best for me. But she can be a little cheeky at times, and she especially likes to be in charge when you're handling her on the ground. She's good in the stable, though, and is very friendly and loves cuddles!

Her sassy nature can come through out hacking, too, and she'll test her rider by pretending to be spooky. I know that she's putting it on and isn't really scared of anything, though!

DID YOU KNOW?

Flora had a foal called Mowgli through embryo transfer, and I'm hoping he's a star of the future! You can find out more about him on p34!

DID YOU KNOW?

Her best movements are passage and flying changes, although she's pretty talented at all the Grand Prix moves.

We need to be in perfect harmony
to ride the moves spot on

ALL THE RIGHT *moves*

Can you spot a piaffe from a passage? Here's some insider info on Grand Prix dressage moves and how we ride them to score top marks

One of the best things about riding at Grand Prix level is that I get to teach my horses to perform all kinds of impressive moves! It can take several years to train them, but it's worth it when we can show them off at a competition. Both horse and rider need to be in total harmony to perform the moves perfectly, so it's important we understand each other and have great communication, too. Want to know all about my fave movements? Here's my guide on what they are, and what I do to impress the judges!

HALF-PASS

What it looks like: When a highly trained horse performs half-pass it'll look like he's gliding effortlessly from one side of the arena to the other! He'll travel on a diagonal line, moving forwards and sideways at the same time, with his outside legs crossing in front of his inside legs. His head will be slightly flexed in the direction he's travelling, and his shoulders should be just ahead of his quarters. It's a move that can be performed in trot or canter.

To get top marks: To wow the judges I need to make sure my horse stays in a lovely rhythm all the way through the half-pass. Every crossing step he takes should be even, and the bend in his body must stay the same, too. He'll also be perfectly balanced and have loads of impulsion that'll make him look like he's springing off the ground!

PIROUETTE

What it looks like: When you think of a dressage horse dancing, the pirouette's sure to be the first move that comes to mind! It's when his front end turns around his quarters, with his hindlegs moving on the spot and making as small a circle as possible. Pirouettes are ridden in walk or canter, and can either be a half turn of 180° or a really impressive full circle.

To get top marks: A perfect pirouette is all in the preparation, and I need to collect my horse's pace before I ask him to start turning. While we're circling I focus on keeping the tempo of his steps the same, so he doesn't suddenly speed up or slow down. He shouldn't stop or step backwards, either. The judge will also want to see some jump in this strides so he really lifts his shoulders as he twirls around.

DID YOU KNOW?
Full canter pirouettes take six to eight strides to complete, and a half-pirouette only three or four.

PIAFFE

What it looks like: Piaffe is an impressive move where the horse trots on the spot. As in a normal trot he'll lift his legs in diagonal pairs, but will return them to the ground again without moving forward – or maybe just inching ahead a little. You'll notice his hindquarters are lower than his front end, which is because they're taking more of his weight and providing the power needed for the movement.

To get top marks: The judge will be watching very closely that my horse's steps are the right height and, as with all dressage moves, that he stays in a rhythm and has lots of energy. His movement should be light and balanced. The number of steps he takes is important, too – I'll need to ride 10 or 11 to achieve a high mark.

DID YOU KNOW?

It's not just the quality of the piaffe that counts. The transitions in and out of it are scored separately and are worth lots of marks!

PASSAGE

What it looks like: Passage is a super-slow trot with lots of collection and elevation, which means the horse's trot steps are short but very high. It's similar to piaffe, but in passage the horse keeps moving forward and it'll look like he's hopping from stride to stride!

To get top marks: You know you're getting passage right when the moment of suspension – the point in trot where all four of the horse's feet are off the ground – lasts much longer than in his regular trot. I'm also aiming for a clear and exaggerated flexion in his knees and hocks, which he should lift very high, showing what's called cadence.

DID YOU KNOW?

The more lead changes you ask for, the more advanced the movement becomes. So a one-time change is way more challenging than a four-time one.

TEMPI CHANGES

What it looks like: Tempi changes are when the horse performs flying changes in quick succession. In a test you may be asked to change lead every four, three, two or one canter strides. It looks a bit like he's skipping!

To get top marks: I have to make sure I'm really accurate and that every flying change is spot on. It's also important to keep count as the judges will notice if I ride too many or too few strides between each one! For the highest marks I need to make sure my horse keeps moving forward in a great rhythm and with lots of energy.

On the LEVEL

Be in the know about all the levels of dressage

If you're thinking about having a go at dressage, but don't quite know where to start, here's my guide to all the test levels and which movements they involve…

Intro

If you've never done dressage before, this is the perfect place to begin! You only need to walk and trot, and the tests are super-simple to help ease you and your pony in gently. Some of the things to brush up on before you compete include centre lines, 20m circles and free walk on a long rein.

DID YOU KNOW?

Some tests take place in a 20x40m arena, but others are ridden in a long, 20x60m arena. Long arena tests start at Prelim, but are more common as you go up the levels.

Prelim

Some riders choose to start at this level if they're confident in walk, trot and canter. The easier Prelim tests are pretty straightforward, and include lots of work on the track and large shapes like 20m circles. However, there are new challenges to master, too, including three-loop serpentines.

Novice

These tests ask you and your pony a few more questions, plus movements and transitions come up a little quicker, too. There's more opportunity to do long arena tests, and you may be asked to ride 10m circles or encourage your pony to take more powerful, medium trot strides. Some Novice tests even introduce you to counter-canter, which is where the outside leg leads, rather than the inside leg!

Elementary

If your pony aces Novice tests, you could step up to Elementary level. There'll be more counter-canter, plus simple changes, where you change canter lead through walk. As well as opening up your pony's stride, you'll ask him to take shorter, more collected steps in walk, trot and canter. Lateral work also makes an appearance in some of the higher numbered Elementary tests, with a few steps of leg-yield part of the challenge!

Medium

Things start to increase in technical difficulty, and more lateral work appears at Medium level. This includes shoulder-in and travers (quarters-in) in trot, plus half-pass in trot and canter. Half walk pirouettes are also included in some tests, and your pony will need to be able to show an impressive extended trot, too! Entering at A in canter's also a requirement in some of the tests, and the judge will want to see you halt and salute straightaway at X.

Advanced Medium

This bridges the gap between Medium and Advanced tests, and is the perfect stepping stone for riders who want to keep moving through the levels. If you get this far you'll encounter more challenging lateral work, and will need to be able to ask your pony to make a flying change. This is an impressive move where you switch canter lead in mid-air! You'll be expected to perform half-pirouettes in canter, too.

Advanced

Riders who are prepared to take on this degree of dressage difficulty will encounter some super-intricate moves. Their horse must be perfectly balanced and supple enough to perform half 5m circles, and they'll be introduced to tempi-changes. These are where you change canter lead through flying changes every three or four strides!

Prix St Georges

Any rider who enters the arena at Prix St Georges (PSG) level has come a long way, and it's the beginning of the international levels of dressage! They'll really look like they're dancing as they perform half pirouettes, half-pass and tempi-changes at an even higher level. Horses must be very established in their training, and have to be at least seven years old to compete at PSG.

Intermediate I and II

The next steps on the dressage journey are Intermediate I and II tests. They're designed to help develop the skills needed for Grand Prix, which is the pinnacle of dressage. Similar moves are included to PSG, but the level of difficulty is increased. So, riders might perform zig-zags in canter half-pass, and ride two-time changes, where you change canter lead every other stride.

Grand Prix

If you've got this far, you've really made it! It's dressage at the very highest level and its where you'll see all the fancy moves like piaffe, passage and flying changes every stride! It takes many years to train a horse to this level of dressage and is an incredible achievement.

FEELING *free*

Create an awesome free walk

Free walk is included in dressage tests at every level, and it's when you give your pony a longer rein and encourage him to stretch out his neck and back. It might seem like an opportunity for you both to have a bit of a breather part-way through your test, but it's really important you keep riding forwards if you want to score the best marks possible!

HOW TO RIDE IT

1. This move's often ridden on a diagonal line to change the rein, and you'll start by turning across the arena at the correct letter. Just before you turn, start to let out your reins so your pony's already in free walk.
2. As you come onto the diagonal, gradually allow your pony a little more rein, so he takes his nose forward and down, but keep a soft contact on his mouth. It should feel like he's taking your hands forward, and he shouldn't drop the reins or curl his head towards his chest.
3. Wrap your legs around his sides to encourage him to stretch out his neck and keep him marching forward with long, active steps. You want him to overtrack, so his hind feet step further than the prints left by his front feet. Make sure he's straight and aiming for the correct letter, too!
4. As you approach the track, calmly shorten your reins until they're at a normal dressage length again. Hug your pony with your legs so he transitions to taking shorter steps without losing that lovely rhythm.

FINE-TUNE YOUR FLATWORK

Fault: My pony doesn't stretch down when I release the rein contact.
Fix it: Gently vibrate your fingers on your reins to massage the bit in his mouth. It'll help keep him focused on you, and encourage him to drop his head and neck and take his nose forward.

Fault: My pony doesn't open up his stride and march forward.
Fix it: Use your hips to encourage your pony to really step out by moving them one at a time, pushing them towards your hand on the opposite side. Having your hands a little forward can help, too, but don't forget to keep a contact with his mouth.

Fault: When I pick up the rein contact at the end of a free walk my pony always jogs.
Fix it: Make sure you take back the reins gradually and smoothly. If you grab or pull them, it'll make him tense up, which could be what's causing him to run forward. Also, if you ride through the test a lot at home, he could start anticipating what comes next, so try practising your free walk in a different place around the school, or don't always go into trot straight after it. This will keep him guessing, so he's always listening for your next instruction.

top tip

Try practising free walk out hacking. You may find your pony has more motivation to march forward when he's out in the open and away from the arena.

TACK ROOM tour

Take a sneak peak into the yard's tack room

Our tack room's probably the busiest place on the yard, and there's people coming and going all the time. They'll be fetching saddles and bridles or rugs, cleaning tack or grabbing a well-earned cup of tea. It's a popular place with the dogs, too! With so much activity it can soon get a bit messy, but I always make sure it's clean and tidy by the end of the day!

Wall of fame
Carl and I have competed at shows all around the world, and we're always given a commemorative plaque that we display on the wall of the tack room. Looking at these always brings back some great memories.

Talking tack
The tack room's wall-to-wall saddles and bridles – well, we do have 20 horses who are ridden every day! There's a mountain of girths, saddle pads and rugs, too.

I'm often busy riding or teaching, but I'll help with the chores if I can. I'm pretty good at tack cleaning, having done an awful lot of it in my life!

Treat time
Right outside the tack room is an area where the horses are groomed and tacked up or untacked, then washed off after they've been ridden. It's so much easier than carrying kit backwards and forwards to the stables.

It's one of the horses' fave places because it's where the sugar lumps are kept. They always get one as a reward after a hack or schooling session.

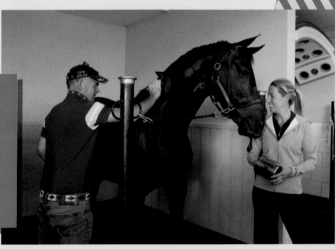

> If I'm not busy riding or teaching
> I'll help out with the chores

ARE YOU *Gold medal* READY?

Find out if you've got what it takes to go for gold with my fab quiz!

Do you dream of becoming a top level rider and taking home a gold medal one day? Well, being a winner requires lots of hard work, patience and dedication, so have a go at my quiz to find out if you've got what it takes to become a champion!

1. Which of these are you most likely to be doing at the yard?

a) Working hard to complete all my jobs at the speed of light – I've got plans later that I can't miss!
b) Making sure my pony and tack are sparkling – it's all about those finishing touches!
c) Planning my training sessions for the rest of the week ahead – got to reach those goals!

2. What's your favourite thing about hacking?

a) I couldn't pick, I just love getting out of the arena!
b) Being able to clear my head and relax.
c) Riding across different terrain to improve my pony's balance and fitness.

3. Do you like having your dressage test called for you?

a) Yes, I never have time to learn it by heart!
b) Occasionally, it depends how well I've memorised it.
c) No need, I always know it inside out.

4. How often do you like to school your pony?

a) Every now and then. I don't like to get too bogged down with flatwork.
b) At least once a week.
c) Three to four times every week – no train, no gain!

5. How important are your riding lessons to you?

a) I look forward to them, but sometimes I just want to have fun with my pony and miss out all the boring bits.
b) Lessons are great fun and I enjoy learning new exercises I can practise with my pony.
c) They're absolutely essential and I'd never go a week without one! I love to spend time perfecting what my instructor has shown me in between lessons, so I can get closer to moving up a level.

6. What would your dream horsey job be?

a) Something that would allow me to help lots of ponies and their owners, like a physio or saddle fitter.
b) I'd like to use my pony know-how to help people reach their goals by being a trainer or sports psychologist.
c) My dream career is to be a professional rider so I can get the best out of lots of different horses.

7. How do you deal with setbacks?

a) I'm not too worried about making mistakes, I just want to have fun with my pony!
b) It's disappointing, but I try to see it as an opportunity to improve for next time.
c) I take setbacks seriously, but I don't let them get me down. I'm disciplined enough to make a plan with my instructor and get myself back on track.

8. In an ideal world, how often would you compete?

a) Probably around once a month or so.
b) Every fortnight, maybe with a couple of extra shows thrown in if things are going well!
c) Every week, and maybe some evening shows, too, but I think I might need another pony or two for that!

9. Where do you see yourself as a rider in five years?

a) I want to be enjoying myself to the max! It would be nice to bring home a few rosettes and do some more unaffiliated competitions.
b) I hope I'll be competing at affiliated level and maybe even be good enough to reach the regional champs!
c) My aim is to break into the higher levels as a serious competitor. I'm willing to work really hard so I can reach the top of my game!

10. Is winning important?

a) Not really, as long as I've done my best and had an awesome time with my pony!
b) Winning is something to strive for, but I'm just happy to be placed.
c) Going for the win is a huge, if not the biggest, part of my motivation.

Mostly As – Bronze medallist
3RD

You're a keen rider who loves having fun in the saddle! You enjoy competing, but have a laid-back attitude and like to balance competition success with hanging out with friends and other commitments, too. Even though you're passionate about your pony, you've got the best of both worlds as you're a great competitor, but know it's not the be-all and end-all if you don't come first!

Mostly Bs – Silver medallist
2ND

You're pretty serious about competing and put in the prep to make sure you always do your best! Making progress with your pony is hugely rewarding to you and you love getting the chance to show off your skills. Being placed is proof of your hard work, but clinching a win is a bonus. Getting to the next level will mean booking yourself a few more lessons, so you can make a plan with your instructor that'll help you achieve those dressage dreams!

Mostly Cs – Gold medallist
1ST

You sleep, eat and breathe dressage competitions and coming away with a red rosette is your ultimate aim! Your training plans are focused and effective, your passion and dedication to riding is second to none, and your dream's to become just as good as the world's top riders! You're sure to have your next riding goal in mind, whether that's another championship to aim for, or training an exciting new pony to be a superstar. You never know, you could even find yourself competing against me one day!

EXPLORE
the great outdoors

Discover why hacking can benefit every horse, even an Olympic champion!

There's a good chance hacking is a big part of your riding routine – and if it isn't, it's definitely worth taking the time to do more! From improving your pony's fitness to introducing him to new sights and sounds, hacking ticks so many boxes. Here are a few ways you can get more from the great outdoors.

1. And relax...

Our horses are ridden in the arena four days a week, but every Wednesday they go for a long hack in groups. It's a chance for them to chill out with their friends and have a well-earned break from their busy schooling sessions. It doesn't matter if they're a young horse just starting out in dressage, an established Grand Prix horse or a retired Olympic champion, they all go out hacking!

DID YOU KNOW?
Going for a hack can help you to unwind, too, and it's the perfect way to spend quality time with your pony.

2. Let's explore

You can add even more variety to your pony's schedule by mixing up the hacking routes you take. Sometimes I like to focus on roadwork, but we're lucky that we can ride around the yard's fields, where there's plenty of space to up the pace and have a trot and canter. Going somewhere new will make hacking even more fun for your pony, and he'll enjoy having a change of scenery.

3. Keep him fit

Working your pony in the arena is like taking him to lift weights in the gym – it helps him build up strength and muscle. Out on a hack you can focus on his cardio fitness, which strengthens his heart and improves his stamina. Hill and canter work are both great for increasing his fitness, plus it'll give you a workout, too!

top tip

Going on different hacks introduces your pony to loads of new things, which can help make him less spooky at shows.

top tip

If you want to build your pony's fitness, speak to your parents and instructor about taking him to a local gallops. This is a long stretch of sand or grass where you can do some dedicated canter work.

4. School as you go

You don't need to confine your pony's learning to the arena – you can school him while out hacking as well! There's so many useful things you can do, including riding lots of transitions, asking him to lengthen his stride and practising leg-yield. Make sure you only school him on a bridleway, where it's safe, though, and not on the roads or near traffic. Plus, always check the path's clear of walkers or cyclists before you start going sideways!

5. Wind down slowly

Cooling down our horses after a schooling session is really important to help prevent them getting sore muscles. Sometimes we do this on a short hack instead of in the arena. It's the perfect way to reward the horses for working hard, and it means they can relax and walk out on a loose rein while stretching out their neck and back muscles. Why not try this cool-down routine with your own pony?

BE SAFE, BE SEEN!

Whether you're riding on the roads or hacking out on a bridleway, it's super-important that both you and your fave pony wear hi-vis. On the roads it'll help motorists see you up to three seconds sooner, so they can slow down. Off-road it'll make you more visible to walkers and cyclists, and even low-flying aircraft. Another really good reason to wear hi-vis is that if you and your pony part company, it should be much easier to find you!

WORDSEARCH

Can you find all the dressage themed words hidden in the grid?

H	G	E	P	P	A	T	E	S	T	B	B	S	I	A	H
Q	Z	R	G	I	J	F	D	N	K	E	P	E	W	V	Z
G	K	O	E	W	R	R	A	C	M	N	M	L	H	U	L
D	U	L	V	E	G	O	L	Y	I	I	F	D	V	R	C
I	T	Y	C	S	U	M	U	D	G	L	W	E	A	O	P
A	X	M	T	S	I	O	X	E	M	E	W	C	L	R	A
G	I	P	W	G	L	K	J	Q	T	R	F	N	E	F	H
O	R	I	X	T	F	E	P	O	E	T	R	I	G	U	A
N	P	A	J	S	R	D	I	G	T	N	E	J	R	D	L
A	D	D	K	S	E	I	A	S	H	E	P	C	O	L	T
L	N	R	I	T	E	S	F	Q	L	C	M	I	D	I	K
R	A	R	G	T	S	A	F	H	N	B	G	V	E	H	J
K	R	P	T	E	T	L	E	U	M	X	N	E	J	O	L
C	G	W	R	U	Y	B	B	L	U	E	B	E	R	R	Y
S	C	D	J	I	L	R	Y	G	L	U	V	H	S	B	S
I	B	T	B	C	E	N	H	A	L	F	P	A	S	S	M

TEST YOURSELF

Have a go at designing your very own dressage test!

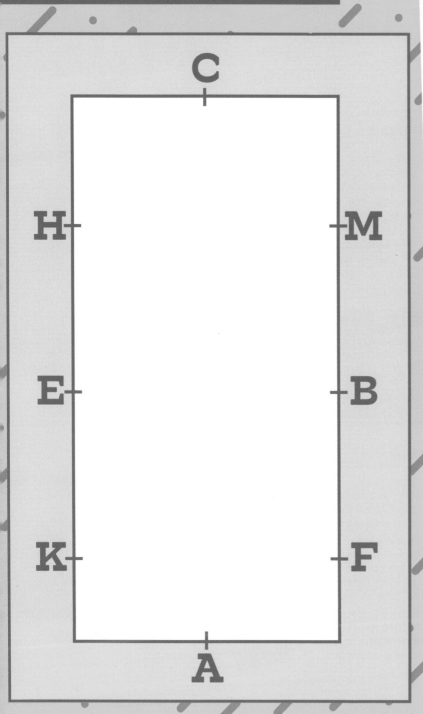

C

H **M**

E **B**

K **F**

A

What to do
If you've been inspired by all the amazing things you're reading about dressage in this Yearbook, why not have a go at designing your very own test? You can make it as easy or as challenging as you like, then ride it through on your fave pony! Use the arena diagram here to help you.

top tip

Use different coloured pencils or pens to show walk, trot and canter.

NOTES ....
....
....

POWER UP

How to ride medium trot

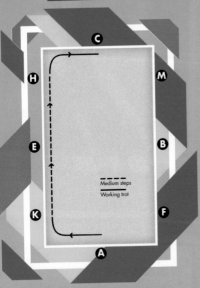

Medium steps
Working trot

If you want to really add the wow factor to your pony's paces, teach him to take bigger, more powerful steps. These are called medium strides and can be ridden in trot, and also in canter when you're more experienced. The important thing is that your pony goes forward with more energy, but he doesn't get faster or lose the rhythm. Here's what you need to do...

top tip
You can also ask your pony to take longer strides in walk, which is called extended walk.

HOW TO RIDE IT

1. Go large on the left or right rein in working trot and make sure your pony's going forward with lots of energy.
2. Ride past A and through the corner, then rebalance him by asking for a half-halt. This is when you take a soft feel on the reins to ask him to wait, then immediately ride forward again.
3. Now ride for those bigger, more powerful strides! To do this, squeeze him with your legs to encourage him forward, and allow a little with your hands so he can lift his neck and head. Remember,

though, to keep a steady, even contact on your reins.
4. Make things easy for your pony at first by just asking him for one or two bigger steps before coming back to a working pace. You can then build up gradually and try for a few more medium steps at a time.
5. Change the rein and try the other way.
6. When your pony's got the hang of medium trot on the long side, have a go across the diagonal. Come out of the corner, rebalance him with a half-halt, and make sure he's straight before asking for extra energy.

FINE TUNE YOUR FLATWORK

Fault: When I ask for bigger steps my pony loses balance and falls onto his forehand.
Fix it: Try riding half-halts to set your pony up for the transition. They'll make sure he's balanced and will encourage him to bring his hindlegs underneath him so he can power forward. Remember to support him with your position, too, by sitting up tall with your shoulders back.

Fault: My pony just gets faster, rather than taking longer strides.
Fix it: To avoid your pony racing off, aim to ride a really smooth transition from the working to the medium pace by using light and subtle aids. Don't suddenly clap your legs against his sides as this will just encourage him to run forward.

DID YOU KNOW?
To be a true medium pace, your pony must overtrack. This means his hind feet should stretch even further forward than the prints that are left by his front feet.

top tip
Check your pony's taking longer strides by counting how many steps he takes between two markers in working and medium trot. In medium he'll cover the distance in fewer strides.

TRAVEL
in style

Why the lorry's so much more than a way to get from A to B

We spend a lot of time on the road travelling to shows, so the lorry's like a second home to us. When we're away it's my sanctuary – it's where I sleep, where I get ready for competitions and the place I go to chill out before I ride. It's also where we celebrate when things have gone well!

> The lorry's like a second home to us and is my sanctuary when we're away

DID YOU KNOW?
The lorry can carry up to six horses.

Home comforts

I've kitted out the living area with some cute cushions that have different horsey designs. I absolutely love them – they're pretty and comfy and make the lorry feel even more like home.

DID YOU KNOW?

What music we listen to in the lorry depends on whether we need livening up or chilling out!

No dogs allowed!

I'm a clean freak and do my best to keep the lorry living area tidy. The dogs aren't usually allowed in here, but they try and sneak in when I'm not looking. I'm always banning Alan, too, because he drops shavings everywhere!

DID YOU KNOW?

My absolute fave lorry snack is Percy Pigs sweets.

Pack it in

Before we head off to a show, the lorry's packed carefully to make sure we have everything we need. Our tack's put into trunks, which are carried in and stored in the middle section of the lorry, between the horses and the living area. As well as all our usual gear, we'll take spares of everything. From reins and bits to girths and horseshoes, we have extras in case anything breaks or goes missing.

When we fly to a show, we can only take the essentials, so it's really important we don't forget anything! I really miss having the lorry at far-away shows, but we always book an extra stable to use as a chill-out zone, and to store all our snacks in!

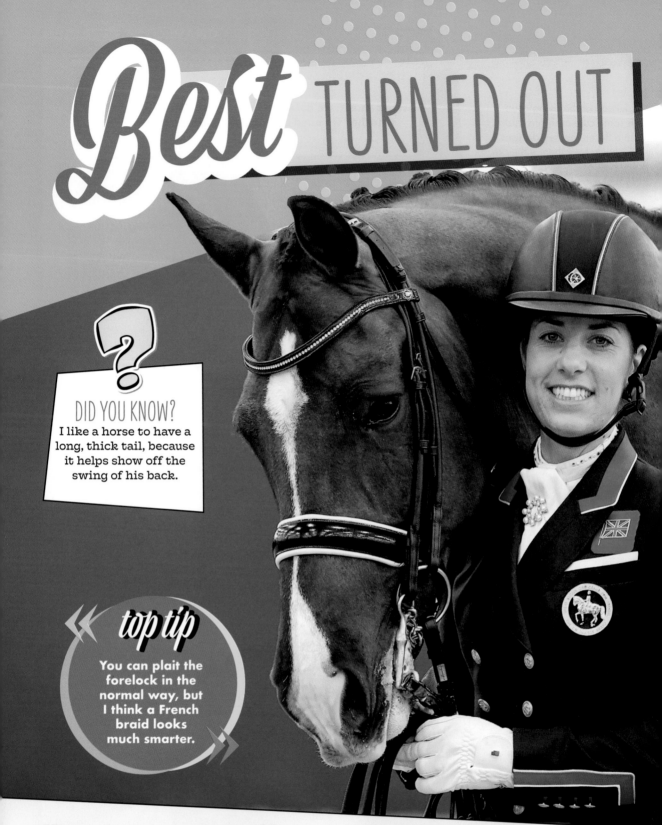

Best TURNED OUT

?

DID YOU KNOW?

I like a horse to have a long, thick tail, because it helps show off the swing of his back.

top tip

You can plait the forelock in the normal way, but I think a French braid looks much smarter.

Here's how our groom Alan makes my horses look amazing

I'm so lucky that I have super-groom Alan Davies to look after my horses. Not only is he brilliant at getting them gleaming for major competitions, he gives them all the best care possible, whether they're on the yard or far away from home at an international show. He's given me the OK to share some of his grooming secrets with you, so here are his tips for creating eye-catching quarter marks and plaiting your pony to perfection!

Making your mark

Quarter marks add the perfect finishing touch to a competition horse's turnout. As well as looking great, they show off the hindquarters and enhance his conformation. When Valegro turned down the centre line at the Olympics, he had patriotic half Union Jack quarter marks. It's a design you can easily recreate on your pony's coat, too! Here's what to do...

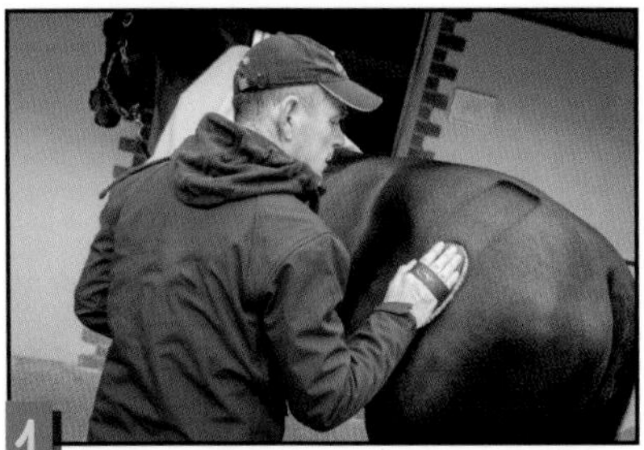

1 Take a slightly damp water brush and run it down the middle of your pony's quarters to create a vertical line. Keep going until you're level with the point of his hip.

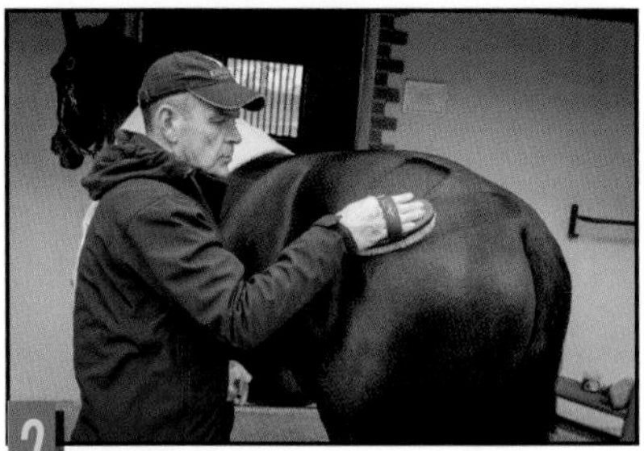

2 Place your brush on the top of your pony's quarters, just above his dock. Now sweep it in a diagonal line until it meets the bottom of your vertical stripe.

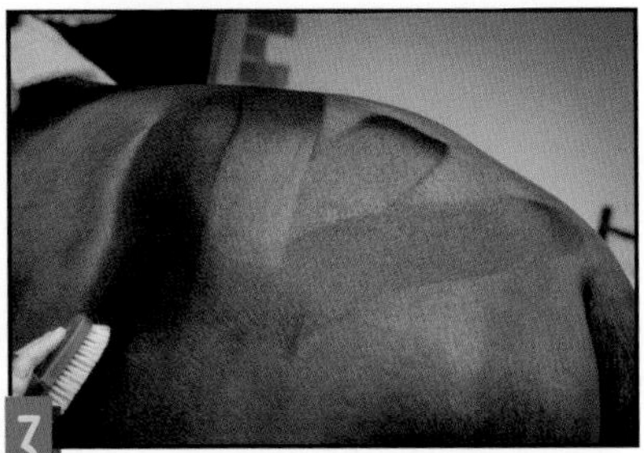

3 Create another diagonal line, this time to the left of your middle stripe. Try to make sure that all three lines are evenly spaced at the top.

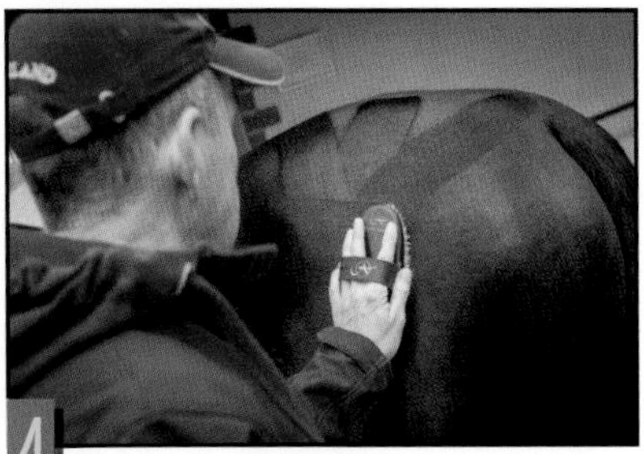

4 To complete your half Union Jack, take your brush and sweep it in a horizontal line along the bottom of your design.

5 Now mirror the pattern on the other side. To help you make sure the designs are even on both sides, find something safe to stand on so you can look down onto this hindquarters from above.

top tip

Before applying quarter marks, brush your pony's coat so it's free from dust.

Roll with it

It's correct to plait up for dressage competitions, and you're sure to think that professional riders only have sewn-in plaits in their horse's mane. Well, think again! Alan makes our horses' manes look amazing using plaiting bands. Here's how you can follow his quick and easy method yourself...

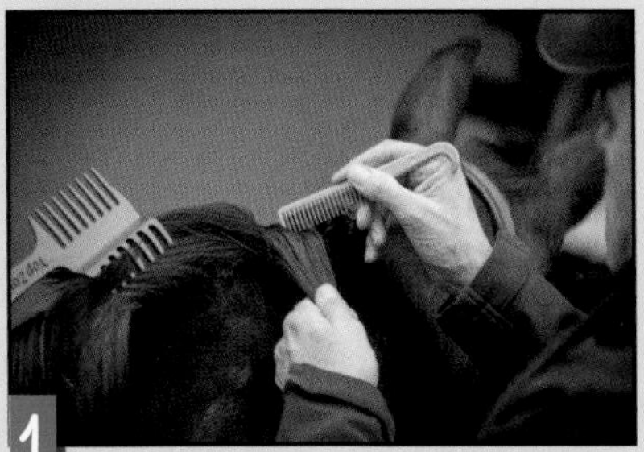

1 Begin by dividing up your pony's mane into equal sections, according to how many plaits you want along his neck. Then take your first section and divide it into three.

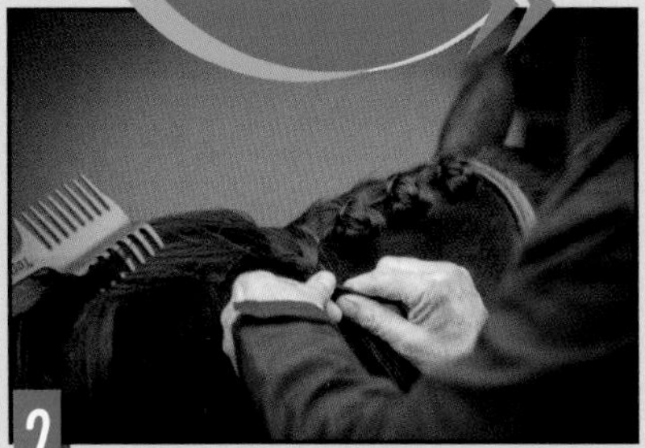

2 Start plaiting. Keep the hair a little loose at the very top, so it doesn't pull on his crest, then braid it a little tighter as you go further down. Plait all the way to the end of the hair.

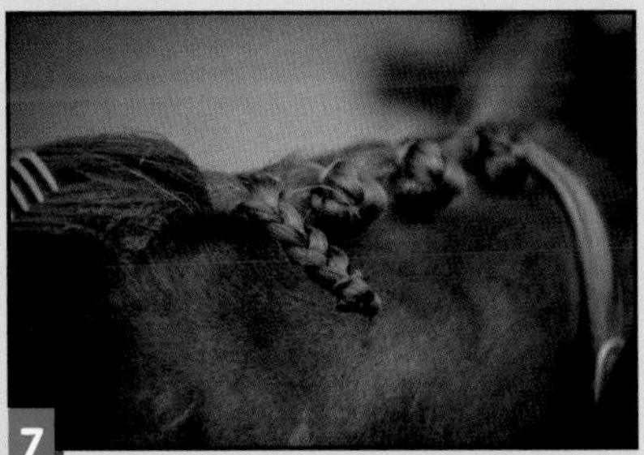

3 Turn the very end of the plait over and wrap a band around it, making sure you don't leave any wispy bits sticking out.

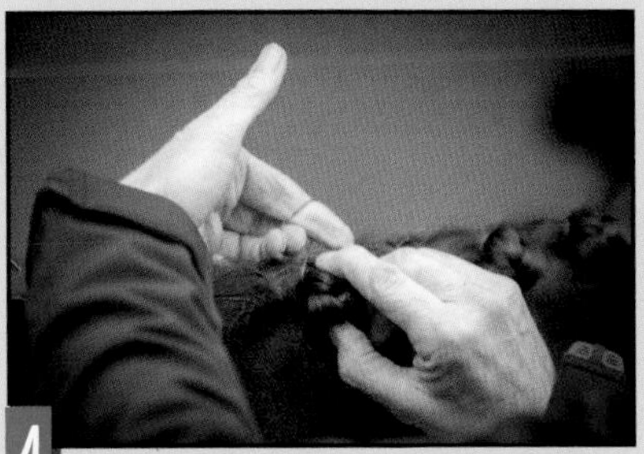

4 Take another plaiting band and twist it around the end. Then, holding the rest of the band above the plait, roll the mane up.

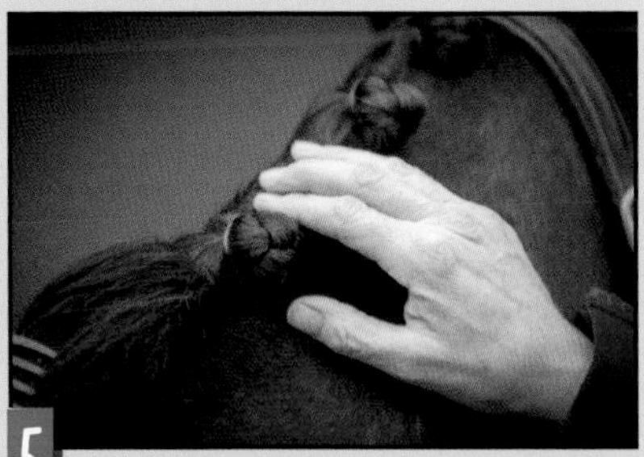

5 When you've rolled your plait up to your pony's crest, twist the band around it. Finish by tucking the band underneath the plait, out of sight.

ARE YOU MY No.1 FAN?

Test what you know about me in this super-fun quiz

1 When I was a child, I competed at Horse of the Year Show in...

A Mounted games

B Showjumping

C Showing

2 What's my star sign?

A Cancer

B Libra

C Aries

3 Which film's soundtrack did I use for some of my dressage to music performances with Valegro?

A Aladdin

B How to Train Your Dragon

C Trolls

4 I have two middle names, but do you know what they are?

A Mary Jane

B Susan Jane

C Claire Louise

5 How old was I when I competed in my first showjumping competition?

A Three

B Five

C Seven

DID YOU KNOW?

I appeared in the festive finale at Olympia when I was a child. It was so much fun!

6 At which competition did I win my first ever dressage medal with Valegro?

A 2011 European Championships

B 2012 Olympic Games

C 2013 European Championships

7 Which super-popular horsey TV show did I make a guest appearance on?

A Heartland

B Spirit Riding Free

C Free Rein

9 My biography was published in 2017 – what's it called?

A The Girl on the Dancing Horse

B The Girl with Three Gold Medals

C The Girl with the Beautiful Horses

11 Valegro and I hold the world record for the highest ever freestyle dressage score – but what is it?

A 83.663%

B 93.857%

C 94.3%

8 What do I have named after me in my home town of Enfield?

A Houses

B Leisure centre

C Park

10 Which item of clothing do I wear to bring me luck at competitions?

A Jacket

B Breeches

C Socks

12 If I'm ever lucky enough to get some down time, what will you find me watching on TV?

A Reality shows

B Documentaries

C Dramas

TURN TO PAGE 84 FOR THE ANSWERS →

How many did you get right?

1-5 You're off to a great start! All you need to do now is read this Yearbook from cover to cover, then you'll know a few more fabulous facts about me.

6-9 I'm so impressed. You have a pretty sound knowledge about me, and are just a few steps away from being a super-fan. This Yearbook will help take you to the next level!

10-12 Wow, go to the top of the class! You really can claim the title of being my number one fan as you know pretty much everything about me and my dressage career.

I SCORED

Set THE SCORE

Writing down your dressage scores is a brilliant way to chart your progress and you can look back and see how far you've come. Use these pages to record your results, and choose one thing to work on from each test that'll help you improve your performance next time out!

Date: ....

Venue: ....

Test: ....

Percentage: ....

Placing

Fave judge's comment:

....

....

....

What to work on: ....

....

....

....

....

Date: ....

Venue: ....

Test: ....

Percentage: ....

Placing

Fave judge's comment:

....

....

....

What to work on: ....

....

....

....

Date: ....

Venue: ....

Test: ....

Percentage: ....

Placing

Fave judge's comment:

....

....

....

What to work on: ....

....

....

....

Date: ....

Venue: ....

Test: ....

Percentage: ....

Fave judge's comment:

Placing

....

....

....

What to work on: ....

....

....

....

Date: ....

Venue: ....

Test: ....

Percentage: ....

Fave judge's comment:

Placing

....

....

....

What to work on: ....

....

....

....

Date: ....

Venue: ....

Test: ....

Percentage: ....

Fave judge's comment:

Placing

....

....

....

What to work on: ....

....

....

....

Date: ....

Venue: ....

Test: ....

Percentage: ....

Fave judge's comment:

Placing

....

....

....

What to work on: ....

....

....

....

Answers

PAGE 72 WORDSEARCH

```
H G E P P A T E S T B B S I A H
Q Z R G I J F D N K E P E W V Z
G K O E W R R A C M N M L H U L
D U L V E G O L Y I I F D V R C
I T Y C S U M U D G L W E A O P
A X M T S I O X E M E W C L R A
G I P W G L K J Q T R F N E F H
O R I X T F E P O E T R I G U A
N P A J S R D I G T N E J R D L
A D D K S E I A S H E P C O L T
L N R I T E S F Q L C M I D I K
R A R G T S A F H N B G V E H J
K R P T E T L E U M X N E J O L
C G W R U Y B B L U E B E R R Y
S C D J I L R Y G L U V H S B S
I B T B C E N H A L F P A S S M
```

PAGE 80
No.1 FAN QUIZ

1 c	7 c
2 a	8 a
3 b	9 a
4 b	10 b
5 a	11 c
6 a	12 a

Blueberry

Gio